Withdrawn

THE GREAT SPHINX

✧ ENDURING MYSTERIES ✧

KEN KARST

Published by
CREATIVE EDUCATION and CREATIVE PAPERBACKS

P.O. Box 227, Mankato, Minnesota 56002
Creative Education and Creative Paperbacks are imprints of The Creative Company
www.thecreativecompany.us

Design by Danny Nanos of Gilbert & Nanos
Production by Joe Kahnke
Art direction by Rita Marshall
Printed in China

Photographs by Alamy (age footstock, Glass Plate, National Geographic Creative, Photo 12, robertharding), Creative Commons Wikimedia (Mstyslav Chernov; David P/Flickr; Jean-Léon Gérôme/Art Renewal Center; Jean Housen/ JMCC1; The New York Times; Marie-Lan Nguyen; Olaf Tausch/Tpt; Elihu Vedder/Museum of Fine Arts, Boston; Wayne77), Getty Images (-/AFP/Stringer, Patrick CHAPUIS/Gamma-Rapho, DEA/G. DAGLI ORTI/De Agostini, FPG/ Hulton Archive Photos, Barry Iverson/The LIFE Images Collection, Rolls Press/Popperfoto), iStockphoto (Goddard_ Photography, powerofforever, Tammy616), NASA (NASA/JPL-Caltech/MSSS), Shutterstock (Anton_Ivanov, Svitlana Belinska, Dan Breckwoldt, Burhan Bunardibogdan ionescu, Sakdinon Kadchiangsaen, Matej Kastelic, Ram Kay, nito, Panda Vector, Pavelvosolok, Aleksandr Pobedimskiy, Stefano Tammaro)

Library of Congress Cataloging-in-Publication Data

Names: Karst, Ken, author.
Title: The great sphinx / Ken Karst.
Series: Enduring mysteries.
Includes bibliographical references and index.
Summary: An investigative approach to the curious phenomena and mysterious circumstances
surrounding the Great Sphinx, from historical legends to archaeological findings to hard facts.

Identifiers: LCCN 2017060032
ISBN 978-1-64026-006-1 (hardcover) / ISBN 978-1-62832-557-7 (pbk) / ISBN 978-1-64000-031-5 (eBook)
Subjects: LCSH: Great Sphinx (Egypt)—Juvenile literature.
Classification: LCC DT62.S7 K37 2018 / DDC 932/.2—dc23

CCSS: RI.5.1, 2, 3, 6, 8; RH.6–8.4, 5, 6, 7, 8

First Edition HC   9 8 7 6 5 4 3 2 1
First Edition PBK   9 8 7 6 5 4 3 2 1

CREATIVE EDUCATION • CREATIVE PAPERBACKS

Table of Contents

The young Egyptian prince liked to hunt. He especially liked hunting in the desert around the city where he lived. The vast desert was mostly empty. But three gigantic pyramids filled the horizon. In front of the pyramids was a truly strange figure —a human head sticking out of the sand, wearing the same headdress as a **pharaoh**. One day, the prince grew sleepy while hunting. He curled up on the ground in the shadow of the carved stone figure. There he dreamed that the figure spoke to him. The voice told him to dig away the sand below its head. If he did so, the prince, instead of the prince's brother, would become pharaoh. The prince and his workers revealed that the head in the desert actually sat atop the body of a lion, with its legs and paws extending many feet in front of the head. No one had seen the lion's body for perhaps a thousand years. It had been covered by the desert's drifting sand. The prince became pharaoh. The great stone figure became known as the Great Sphinx, one of the most attractive—and mysterious—man-made figures in the world.

KEEPING ITS SECRETS

Ancient Greek writers made a list of the most spectacular man-made features they had seen in the world they knew. They called them the Seven Wonders. Only one, the Great Pyramid of Giza, remains. Perhaps it survives because it has been guarded for thousands of years by what looks like a stone watchdog: the Great Sphinx.

The Great Sphinx and the Great Pyramid stand about eight miles (12.9 km) from the heart of Cairo, Egypt. Cairo is one of the world's largest cities. The Great Pyramid is visible from the city, even through smog. Like most major cities, Cairo keeps growing. Giza was a separate settlement thousands of years ago. Now it is a suburb of Cairo and the third-largest city in Egypt. On the banks of the Nile River, the cities are about 100 miles (161 km) south of the Mediterranean Sea.

Giza is where the ancient Egyptians buried their kings, queens, and other **dignitaries**. It is famed for its necropolis. A necropolis is a large cemetery. The word combines the Greek *nekros*, which means "dead," with *polis*, or "city." When a dignitary died in the ancient Egyptian capital of Memphis, his or her body was floated on a barge about 12 miles (19.3 km) down the Nile to Giza for burial. The pyramids were the burial places for pharaohs who had become regarded as gods. It's where they were believed to depart this world for the afterlife. There are three major pyramids at Giza and several smaller ones. But there is only one Great Sphinx.

The Giza necropolis also holds the ruins of small temples and other ceremonial shrines. People used these areas to pray for the dead. But what was the Sphinx used for? Why is it there? No one knows. There are no carvings or other markings on the statue that might tell us more about it. It simply sits calmly, facing the sunrise. Its face has almost no expression. It's not revealing its story.

Most **Egyptologists** believe that the Sphinx was shaped about 4,500

The pyramids at Giza in Egypt are the oldest and sole remaining structures of the original Seven Wonders of the World.

The ruins of a small temple, thought to have been built around the same time as the Sphinx, remain in front of the stone guardian.

years ago, in about 2500 B.C., about the same time as the pyramids. A chunk of its right shoulder fell off in 1988. That damage caused some Egyptologists to think the Sphinx might be more than 7,000 years old. Some people argue that differing patterns of erosion on the Sphinx prove that it is older.

The pyramids were built of immense stone blocks, cut and placed by thousands of workers. The Sphinx was mostly carved from a single mound of limestone. Only its paws are made of blocks. The Great Sphinx is similar to the faces of the four United States presidents carved on Mount Rushmore in South Dakota. Its head is about half as tall as those on Mount Rushmore. But it sits atop an enormous body. It has a tail that curves around its right side. It is about 240 feet (73.2 m) long and 66 feet (20.1 m) tall. It is one of the largest single-stone statues in the world. Workers carved it with copper chisels and stone hammers. Its paws extend 56 feet (17.1 m) forward from its chest. The ruins of a small temple stand in front of the paws. The Great

Sphinx rests in a sort of pit, lower than much of the ground around it. The pit was once a quarry. Limestone from the quarry was used to build many of the structures at Giza.

Does the Sphinx look like anyone? That question is difficult to answer, partly because the face doesn't have a nose. One popular story was that French soldiers under Napoleon used the nose for target practice with their cannons during an invasion around 1800. That's not true,

One theory suggests that the Sphinx originally depicted the god Anubis, a jackal that guarded the dead, before being re-carved in Khafre's likeness (opposite).

though, because drawings from the 1700s show it without a nose already. More than 300 years before that, an Arab historian wrote that the nose was removed by order of a religious leader. The leader had been upset that local people had been praying to the Sphinx, asking it to bring them good crops.

The Great Sphinx once had a beard. Egyptian pharaohs wore fake beards. Some scholars believe the beard might have been added after the Sphinx was first carved. They think it wasn't attached well and simply fell off. Pieces of it were found over the centuries in rubble below the Sphinx. Some fragments are now in the British Museum and in Cairo's Egyptian Museum. The Sphinx also was once painted with bright colors. Traces of paint can still be seen on its face.

One of the Great Sphinx's key features is its headdress. The broad, striped drapery over and behind its head, called a *nemes*, was worn by the ancient pharaohs of Egypt. The remains of a stone cobra, which came down over the forehead and was a symbol of **divine** power, are also visible on the Great Sphinx.

The most common opinion is that the Sphinx is the image of the Egyptian pharaoh Khafre, who built the second-largest of the three pyramids at Giza. The Great Sphinx is in front of Khafre's pyramid. But some think the Great Sphinx might be the image of Khafre's father, Khufu. The Greek form of the name Khufu is Cheops. Cheops is known as the builder of the Great Pyramid. In 1996, a police identification expert determined the Sphinx more closely resembled Khafre's older brother, Djedefre.

The word *sphinx* might come from a Greek word meaning "strangle." That in turn is linked to a **mythological** sphinx at Thebes. The sphinx would pose a riddle to travelers: What creature walks on four legs in the morning, two legs in the afternoon, and three in the evening? Anyone who couldn't answer correctly was strangled by the sphinx. Oedipus, the mythical hero, guessed the right answer: a human, who crawls on all fours in childhood, walks tall on two legs in adulthood, and uses a cane in old age. He became king of Thebes, and the sphinx killed itself.

The Arabic name for the Great Sphinx was Abu al-Hawl, or "Father of Terror." Many still call it that. But it hasn't always been a fearsome figure. Some records show that the Sphinx was cleared of sand from about 30 B.C. to A.D. 200. During that time,

Egypt was ruled by the Roman Empire. The Sphinx was a popular gathering place. It was even used as a backdrop for plays.

The Great Sphinx has a stone tablet on its chest. That tablet, known as the Dream **Stela**, contains the story of the prince who, inspired by a dream, came to dig the Sphinx out of the sand that had covered it for centuries. The stela was placed there in about 1400 B.C. People have long believed the Great Sphinx had secret tunnels and storehouses beneath it, some holding writings about the lost civilization of Atlantis. Although some cavities have been found, they've been attributed to both erosion and treasure hunters. No ancient writings or valuables have been discovered.

The Great Sphinx is oddly shaped. Its front legs are too long for its body, and its head is too small. Some scholars say that's because it might have originally been a much larger statue of a lion or other catlike animal. They say it might have been scaled down later and given a human head to honor a pharaoh. But there are no pictures, writings, or other evidence to support—or contest—those ideas.

Ho-Hum, Another Sphinx

Sphinxes are popular figures in Greece and Egypt. They also are honored across Southeast Asia and India. In recent centuries, sphinx statues have been erected in public squares in major cities across Europe. The oldest known sphinx is in Turkey. It is thought to have been made in about 9500 B.C. Sphinxes have the head of a human and the body of a lion. Most are male. But some, like the mythological sphinx at Thebes, are female. Egyptians might have been attracted to the idea of sphinxes because lions were common along the Nile River in Egypt. They represented power and protection. They were also a food source. Some sphinxes have wings on their lion bodies. In Egypt, some had a lion's mane and ears—only the face was human. Most sphinxes are regarded as godlike figures, though not gods themselves. Some sphinxes are shown trampling their enemies. Sphinxes are commonly linked with buildings or monuments. These days, there are also living sphinxes: a sphynx is a breed of cat. The cats are distinctive for being hairless, with large, alien-like eyes. But their skin has colors and markings similar to those on regular cats.

HAMMERS, CHISELS, AND DYNAMITE

Walk through a cemetery, and you will find that nearly every gravestone has a name on it. That is the name of the person or family buried there. Similarly, many of the world's most famous statues and monuments tell us clearly whom they are honoring. Each carving identifies a historical figure, a saint, or a god.

But the Great Sphinx is different. There are no carvings or writings on the figure that might tell us what king or queen it is honoring. Nothing tells us what god it might represent. No words or symbols tell us who built it or when. There is no carved or painted quote to suggest that the figure might be "saying" something.

After it was created, time passed. People and rulers came and went. But no one wrote down the story of how the Great Sphinx had come to be. There was no one left who could remember. Blowing sands drifted up against the figure. In time, the Sphinx was buried up to its neck. It was just a head, popping up strangely above the desert floor like a **periscope**, wearing a headdress, and staring into the sunrise.

Over time, travelers and other people who encountered the Sphinx wrote about it or drew pictures. But there are significant gaps in that record. The Greek historian Herodotus traveled the known world in the fifth century B.C. collecting stories and histories. In Egypt, he interviewed people and wrote about how the pyramids were built. But he never mentioned the Sphinx. How could he have missed it? The head was undoubtedly visible. Did someone not want him to write about it? Would the Sphinx have cursed him? That's another mystery.

We have learned a lot about the Great Sphinx in modern times. Travel has become much easier, so many people have been able to visit it. Scientific

At different times in history, only the Sphinx's head has been visible, yet Herodotus (above) never documented it in his journey through Egypt.

tools have become much more sophisticated. **Archaeologists** can probe deeper with minimal damage. But the Great Sphinx still causes Egyptologists to argue. There are disagreements about who built it, when, and why.

A few things about the Great Sphinx are commonly acknowledged. It is often linked to the ancient Egyptian god Horemakhet, the god of the sun as it rises in the morning sky. The Great Sphinx faces directly east, looking into the sun as it rises on each **solstice** and **equinox**. Could the Sphinx represent the god? That's unlikely, since Egyptians of that time did not build figures of their gods. The pharaohs whose faces the Sphinx most likely represents were themselves regarded as gods. So the Sphinx suggests both the human and the heavenly. Its position is also linked to heavenly creatures. In modern times, on the cross-quarter days exactly between each solstice and equinox, the Sphinx faces the point on the horizon at which the constellation Leo rises. Leo represents a lion—staring back, perhaps, at its own image on Earth, carved in stone.

The Great Sphinx rests in front of Khafre's pyramid. As a result, many attribute its construction to him or to his father Khufu (Cheops). But why aren't there sphinxes in front of the other two immense pyramids at Giza? Khafre was a powerful ruler, but so were many Egyptian pharaohs over the centuries. Was he more concerned than the others about making a mark? Were his pyramid and the Great Sphinx built so that people would remember him? Ancient Egyptians didn't write much history, so we don't really know. But that hasn't stopped people from trying to get answers from the Sphinx itself. People have scraped, dug, and blasted away at the figure for centuries. Some of those efforts have damaged the Sphinx. More recently, some of those damages have been repaired. But some repairs have actually

The Great Sphinx gazes into the sunrise as it appears to stand guard in front of the pyramids.

caused more damage. It's a process that's been repeating itself for centuries, under the guidance of both Egyptians and Europeans.

The first restoration of the Sphinx is attributed to the pharaoh Thutmose IV. The Sphinx had been a disembodied head staring across the desert for as long as anyone could remember in Thutmose's time. Motivated by a dream, Thutmose began digging and ultimately exposed part of the Sphinx's lionlike body. That was around 1400 B.C., about 1,000 years after the Sphinx was first carved. Of course, the desert sand eventually blew back into the pit surrounding the Great Sphinx.

Records show that the sand was again cleared away 1,400 to 1,600 years later. So the Sphinx was fully visible during Roman times. But history repeated itself. Sand refilled the pit. When Napoleon came upon the Sphinx in 1798, it was again only a mysterious head poking out of the sand. Napoleon, who mapped the Giza area, measured the Sphinx's head and neck. Famed (and controversial) Egyptian archaeologist Zahi Hawass credits Napoleon with the first modern effort to gain a scientific perspective of the Great Sphinx.

Italian explorer Giovanni Battista Caviglia probed between the paws of the Sphinx from 1817 to 1819. There he found the Dream Stela and pieces of the Sphinx's beard. From 1840 to 1842, British officer and scholar Howard Vyse blasted a hole with dynamite into the back of the Sphinx. He drove 27 feet (8.2 m) down until his drill became stuck, at which point he abandoned the project. The following year, German archaeologist Karl Richard Lepsius cleared away the temple between the paws. French archaeologist Auguste Mariette, who later founded the Egyptian Museum in Cairo, cleared more sand away from the Sphinx in 1858. He found several stone boxes, which he determined had been monuments to Osiris, a god of the dead. Another French archaeologist, Émile Baraize, directed a project to clear the sands entirely away from Sphinx. That project spanned the years 1925 to 1936. Baraize also bricked up an entrance to the interior of the Sphinx, under its tail, although later work found it led only a few feet to dead ends. Baraize repaired the Sphinx's head, neck, and body with concrete. This was later seen as a mistake that marred the Sphinx's appearance. Further restoration efforts sought to reverse Baraize's work.

In 1925, a huge project was undertaken to clear away sand from the Great Sphinx, exposing it entirely for the first time in centuries.

Few of those researchers, if any, left useful records about their projects or findings. More recent probes of the Sphinx have used sophisticated technology. In 1977, Stanford Research Institute, in cooperation with Ain Shams University in Cairo, used **remote sensing** to search for possible cavities, tunnels, or rooms inside or underneath the Sphinx. Rumors of the existence of such passages had been around for centuries. The project found no such chambers. Since then, Mark Lehner, an American archaeologist who leads an international Egyptian research organization, has developed precise maps of the surface of the Sphinx.

Hawass describes the Great Sphinx as being "under siege." From the 1950s to the 1980s, he says, it was harmed by the use of patching materi-

al that turned out to prevent the underlying rock from "breathing." That caused it to throw off newly applied stones meant to repair ancient damage. Drilling to install light and sound cables also took a toll. By simply surviving into the 21st century, the Sphinx has come to experience numerous troubling developments. Vibrations from aircraft, vehicular traffic, and dynamiting from a nearby limestone quarry can shake the structure and crack it. Dramatic population expansion in the area has brought sewage leaks. Nearby factories have created pollution that causes further damage. "The Sphinx is the oldest patient in the world and needs our constant attention," Hawass says.

The Great Excavator Thutmose IV reigned in Egypt for only eight years. But his influence was far greater than that of many other pharaohs, particularly with regard to the Sphinx. Motivated by a dream (and probably a quest for power), Thutmose led the first effort to clear sand away from the Sphinx in about 1400 B.C. For more than 1,000 years, desert sand had drifted around the Sphinx, leaving only the head aboveground. Thutmose's excavation revealed part of the immense lion's body beneath the head, including the two long forelegs. He had walls built to keep sand from filling back in. But they didn't work. For much of the next 3,000 years, travelers and scholars again came to know the Sphinx by only its head. Thutmose made other marks. As pharaoh, he crushed rebellions in nearby Syria and Palestine. He worked out peace treaties with groups in that region and married a local princess. At Thebes, he finished construction of what became the largest obelisk ever built in Egypt. The 105-foot-tall (32 m) stone pillar was later carted away to Rome, where it still stands. It is known as the Lateran Obelisk.

SEND
A SELFIE!

Travelers, soldiers, and religious pilgrims have passed within view of the Sphinx for centuries. Many sketched the massive figure, which must have been astonishing and extremely strange to them. Most encountered the Sphinx as a colossal head emerging from the sand. In some sketches, it wears a crown or a feather. In others, it has a cape and collar. (There is no archaeological evidence that the Great Sphinx ever bore any such ornament.) Its beard might be curved, as a god's was thought to be in those days.

German traveler Johannes Helferich created a woodcut of the Great Sphinx in 1579. Modern viewers might call it cartoonish. He showed it with prominently female characteristics, reflecting his belief that the statue represented the goddess Isis. She was one of the most important of the Egyptian deities. English traveler George Sandys led a group of people through the Middle East in 1610. An illustration of the Sphinx in his book, *A Relation of a Journey*, was much more detailed and accurate than Helferich's. Other travelers put the Great Sphinx on pictorial maps or landscapes, sometimes showing it as a head bobbing in a rolling sea of sand.

French artist and archaeologist Vivant Denon accompanied Napoleon on his campaign through Egypt. Denon sketched the Great Sphinx, showing it to gaze slightly skyward. A long ladder stands on the sand and extends above the back of the head. Atop the head, three men stand dwarfed by the Sphinx's size.

Photographs of the Great Sphinx date back to the 1800s, when photography was first being developed and improved. One remarkable photo was taken from a hot-air balloon. It shows the entire back of the statue, a rare view for that time. Photos throughout the 1800s show it in various stages of emergence from the sands, thanks to archaeologists' work. One

portrays the Sphinx with its long forelegs partially buried, like a dog playing on the beach. Many later photos include crowds of soldiers or other military figures, as well as tourists, posing along its neck and shoulders.

In 1921, delegates from several countries met in Cairo to decide boundaries for new nations in the Middle East. Many of them ventured out to Giza on camels and had their picture taken in front of the Great Sphinx. One of them was Winston Churchill, who later guided Great Britain through World War II. England is a notoriously cloudy nation. Among the dozen or so people in the photo at the Sphinx, Churchill is the only one wearing sunglasses.

In recent history, the Great Sphinx has been a recurring image on Egyptian money. Today it is on the back of the 100-pound note. That bill is worth about $5.50 in U.S. dollars. The Great Sphinx was also on the back of a form of currency issued in 1899 known as a 50-piastre note. That image showed the Great Sphinx in its desert surroundings.

A full-color replica of the Great Sphinx stands sentry in front of the pyramid-shaped Luxor Hotel & Casino in Las Vegas. It is far from identical to the Great Sphinx: It has a nose. Its nemes has vivid blue- and copper-colored stripes. It has heavy eye makeup. It also has a full beard. It is 110 feet (33.5 m) tall, 45 feet (13.7 m) taller than the original at Giza. It was built in 1993, so it will be a while before the Vegas Sphinx is considered an ancient wonder.

Today, the world-famous Great Sphinx has been replicated at a Las Vegas hotel and displayed on Egyptian currency.

The Great Sphinx has long been a figure in entertainment. The 1933 film *The Sphinx* was a murder mystery that didn't involve Egypt at all. One of the film's main characters, who is both deaf and unable to speak, is represented by the face of the Sphinx. A 1981 film, *Sphinx*, involved a search for a forgotten tomb, a legendary curse, and people dealing in the **black market** of Egyptian **antiquities**. Set in 1934, *Indiana Jones and the Secret of the Sphinx* is one of dozens of books about the famed fictional adventurer and archaeologist. In this title, Jones is searching for the Omega Book, which contains instructions on how to rewrite history—and humanity's fate. The book is buried beneath the Sphinx. That's an idea that came from the American **psychic** Edgar Cayce, who was popular during the early decades of the 20th century. In the novel, Jones gets to the Sphinx but leaves without the Omega Book he was seeking. In Disney's 1992 film *Aladdin*, Aladdin and Jasmine fly past the Great Sphinx on a carpet as a worker is shaping the monument's nose. So surprised is the worker to see these airborne travelers that his hand slips, and the Great Sphinx's nose is accidentally chiseled off. So there's one answer to the Sphinx's many riddles!

In 2016, archaeology met Hollywood when part of a sphinx was excavated from the sand in California's Guadalupe-Nipomo Dunes. It was the last of 21 sphinxes built for the movie *The Ten Commandments*, filmed in 1923. Unlike the Great Sphinx, these sphinxes were only meant to last two months. They were made of plaster and abandoned after filming ended. Some were taken to nearby residents' homes. Two wound up at the entrance of the Santa Maria Golf Course for several years. Remnants of the last model have been taken to the Guadalupe-Nipomo Dunes Center, for public display. The plaster sphinxes were in some ways perfect for the movie. Mov-

Replicas of the Sphinx have appeared in many movies (opposite); psychic Edgar Cayse believed a hidden chamber lay beneath the monument.

ies of that time were entirely silent, and so are the secretive sphinxes.

The Great Sphinx comes alive, in a way, in a video game launched in 2003. In *Sphinx and the Cursed Mummy*, the Great Sphinx gets off its haunches and becomes a sort of superhero. In the game, the Sphinx tries to recover both a legendary sword and four crowns once worn by Egyptian gods. Along the way, it encounters historical Egyptian figures, ancient curses, gods, and other challengers.

American artist Elihu Vedder, born in 1836, was fascinated by mythological images. He lived in Italy for 60 years. Vedder never went to Egypt, but he painted several works with sphinxes that resemble the Great Sphinx. One of them, "The Questioner of the Sphinx," hangs in the Museum of Fine Arts in Boston. It shows a wanderer leaning against the sphinx's lips, as if listening for the answer to a question. The sphinx in the painting is buried up to its chin in sand, much like the Great Sphinx was.

English poet Percy Bysshe Shelley put a desert sphinx at the center of one of his most famous poems, "Ozymandias," published in 1818. Ozymandias was another name for Ramses II, who was perhaps Egypt's most powerful pharaoh. Caviglia found an enormous statue of Ramses II in 1820, near the ruins of Memphis. But Shelley describes the "king of kings" as "half sunk," with "a shattered visage." That sounds a lot like the Great Sphinx at Giza. Shelley goes on to say that an inscription asks passersby to look around and marvel at the ruler's mighty works. But of course, there are none; the desert is otherwise empty. The Great Sphinx stands near the pyramids, which are mighty, indeed. But time and human curiosity have taken their toll on the pyramids and on the Great Sphinx. That is an echo of Shelley's idea that humanity's greatest monuments don't last forever.

The Questioner of the Sphinx, *painted by Elihu Vedder in 1863, portrays a weary traveler waiting for a revelation.*

34

The Sphinx Boss

Zahi Hawass (pictured) is one of the top experts on the Great Sphinx, the pyramids, and other Egyptian cultural icons. He is a sort of icon himself. Hawass is Egypt's former Minister of State for Antiquities Affairs. He earned advanced Egyptology degrees and taught college in the U.S. before being appointed minister in 2011. He quickly left that post when his ally, Egyptian president Hosni Mubarak, was removed from office. As a writer and lecturer, Hawass became an even bigger celebrity. He sponsored a line of Indiana Jones–style clothing and was often featured on the National Geographic Channel discussing new archaeological discoveries. He banned Beyoncé from the pyramids, saying she showed up late for a tour and refused to apologize. He personally escorted U.S. president Barack Obama on a tour of Giza in 2009. He has been accused of profiting personally from his privileged access to Egyptian artifacts. Some even say he allowed artifacts to be stolen. Researchers have said he blocks studies that question the age of the Great Sphinx. But Hawass has also worked to have museums around the world return ancient relics found in and taken from Egypt. So he has been seen as a champion of Egyptian culture.

SCHOLARS AND TERRORISTS

Despite centuries of intense study by scholars from around the world, Egypt contains many mysteries. This situation will probably be permanent, says Egyptologist Thomas Schneider. Thousands of years of flooding by the north-flowing Nile River slowly buried ancient settlements in the northern part of Egypt, where the river empties into the Mediterranean Sea. Much of Egyptian civilization has flourished in that area through the centuries. Flooding was critical to the ancient Egyptians' way of life. It brought water and nutrients into what was mostly an arid land. That helped to grow food. But the flooding also slowly buried many cities and towns with layers of sediment. The ancient royal capital of Sais is a good illustration. In 1828, French archaeologist and **philologist** Jean-François Champollion noted that its ruins looked like the remains of a palace built by giants. Today, nothing is left of them. Flooding along the Nile has been controlled by the Aswan High Dam since 1970. Below the dam, the human population has increased dramatically. Sites and materials that might have had value to archaeologists have been reused and built over without much thought. Between 1960 and 1980, several ancient monuments and sites were relocated—a few were even reconstructed in different countries!—as the Aswan High Dam's reservoir flooded others. This has given Schneider a view of Egyptian antiquities that's different from that of most scholars and tourists. "Egypt represents an archaeological disaster area," he writes.

Wherever there are blanks in the Egyptian archaeological record, some researchers have not hesitated to fill them in with their own opinions. They have popularized ideas that most serious Egyptologists reject. They have asserted that the Great Sphinx and the pyramids were built long before 2500 B.C., when most scholars believe the Great Sphinx was first shaped. Researchers such as Robert Schoch and Graham Hancock suggest that the Great Sphinx and the pyramids were built by an earlier, advanced civilization that later vanished.

Schoch, an associate professor of natural sciences at Boston University, believes that patterns of erosion on the Great Sphinx prove that it is older than is commonly stated. He writes that curving, smooth channels running vertically along the Great Sphinx were made by rainfall. Rainfall was much more common in northern Egypt from the end of the last Ice Age, around 10,000 B.C., to about 3000 B.C. Then the region turned extremely dry, as it is today. Schoch writes that an advanced civilization built the Great Sphinx sometime between 7000 and 5000 B.C. Critics, such as Zahi Hawass, point

Flooding along the Nile and the 1960s construction of the Aswan High Dam necessitated the relocation of such ancient sites as the temple complex of Philae (opposite) and the Abu Simbel temples (above).

out that no other evidence of such a civilization has been found. But Schoch says those earlier people could have been wiped out by some kind of natural disaster, such as a comet or flood. The Great Sphinx's head, oddly small compared with its body and forelegs, used to be bigger, Schoch notes. But, he says, it was re-carved to resemble the pharaoh Khafre in about 2500 B.C.

Hancock is a British writer and researcher. He argues that the Great Sphinx is evidence of a connection between Earth and Mars. Its face, he writes, resembles a form visible on the Martian surface. But Hancock and Robert Bauval, a Belgian author and Egyptologist, also write that the arrangement of the three pyramids and the Great Sphinx represent a map of the heavens showing the stars as they would have appeared over Giza in about 10,500 B.C. The pyramids match the three stars in the belt of the constellation Orion. The Great Sphinx mirrors Leo, the lion-shaped constellation that it would have been facing for an hour before dawn on the spring equinox. Their conclusion: the people who saw that heavenly display in the stars built monuments to reflect it. But that was thousands of years earlier than those who are given the credit by most Egyptologists.

The Great Sphinx and its neighbors, the pyramids, have long been among the most-visited sites in the world. But that has changed in recent years. In 2010, Egypt as a whole was host to 14.7 million tourists. In 2016, that number was down to 5.4 million. Thousands of jobs in the tourism business have been lost. Al Jazeera, the Middle Eastern news agen-

An image recorded by NASA's Curiosity *Mars rover in 2014 revealed a blurry object resembling the Great Sphinx within a Martian crater.*

cy, reported in April 2017 that visiting Giza was "like walking on the moon: it's deserted, forlorn, and uninhabited."

The reasons are obvious. Egypt has recently been the site of frequent wars, rebellions, and terrorism. In 2011, Cairo was the scene of open conflict between the government and thousands of citizens who wanted a more **democratic** system. People died in riots only a few miles from Giza. Two years later, the army threw out the country's first democratically elected president. Then, in 2015, a plane traveling from the popular resort town of Sharm el-Sheikh to St. Petersburg, Russia, was bombed in flight. All 224 people aboard were killed. The terrorist group ISIL (the Islamic State in Iraq and the **Levant**) claimed responsibility. Russia and several other countries temporarily banned flights to and from Egypt. In April 2017, 44 people were killed when suicide bombers attacked 2 Christian churches in Egypt.

Money earned from tourists' visits to famous sites is partly used to help maintain them. If they fall into disrepair, fewer people may want to see them. It may also become more difficult to find the money to pay for security at the sites. If they're considered risky places to visit, people are more likely to stay away.

But a tourism turnaround could be on the way. In March 2017, large parts of a 26-foot-tall (7.9 m) statue of a pharoah were unearthed in the heart of Cairo. The figure was belived to be Psammetich I, who ruled from 664 to 610 B.C. A short time later, the remains of another pyramid, built between 1800 and 1640 B.C., were found at Dahshur, just south of Cairo. Such discoveries could re-energize interest in the area's antiquities.

Anticipated to open in 2018, the Grand Egyptian Museum at Giza was expected to be beneficial to the area. Hailed by some as the "fourth pyramid

Recent riots and political unrest in Egypt have caused concern for public safety in popular tourist areas, including Cairo and nearby Giza.

of Giza," it is reported to be the world's largest archaeological museum.

Preserving the heritage and mystery of the Great Sphinx may require more than just a new museum nearby. Forces are working in the opposite direction. In 2015, the leader of ISIL called for the destruction of the Great Sphinx as well as the pyramids. Abu Bakr al-Baghdadi said his group's followers had a "religious duty" to end people's worship of material objects and idols such as statues and monuments. ISIL, now known more simply as the Islamic State or IS, has blown up, bulldozed, or otherwise destroyed several ancient and historic monuments in Libya, Syria, and Iraq. But the group has also recognized the value that many people place on these monuments. Members have sold historic artifacts from the sites and used the money to buy weapons.

For now, the Great Sphinx continues to gaze over the land. It is unmoved by the events unfolding around it. It remains still beneath the movements of the stars above and the earth below. The Sphinx has stared into the sunrise for at least 4,600 years, revealing nothing of its own story. It will continue to do so well into the uncertain future.

Death Worship? Not Exactly ...

Ancient Egyptians are known for having built the pyramids—tombs so large they can be seen from space. They also perfected the craft of mummification. This process preserved the bodies of the dead by drying them and wrapping them with cloth. This was believed to help the dead person live better in the afterlife. Another belief was that it preserved the body for the soul to return to it later. Does that mean the Egyptians had an unhealthy fascination with death? Did they worship death? Not at all, scholars say. Many claim one reason the Egyptians didn't try to conquer other lands was because they loved their home in the Nile Valley so much. Their chief god was the sun god Ra. That suggests a worship of light, life, and warmth. The Sphinx faces the sunrise, a symbol of hope and new beginnings, rather than the sunset, a symbol of decline and death. Pharaohs who lived long lives were considered gods. Scholars also note that repeated flooding of the Nile wiped out many of the details of Egyptian life. We don't know as much about their everyday activities and celebrations as we do about their burial sites.

A well-known symbol from ancient Egypt, the ankh represented life, both in this life as well as the afterlife.

Field Notes

antiquities: objects, buildings, or works of art from the distant past

archaeologists: people who study human history by examining ancient peoples and their artifacts

black market: the business of illegally buying and selling goods

democratic: controlled by the people; a form of government featuring majority rule

dignitaries: people who are considered important because of their rank or office

divine: coming from, or having to do with, God or a god

Egyptologists: archaeologists or historians, or students of languages or art, who focus on ancient Egypt

equinox: one of the two days each year when the sun rises due east and sets due west, creating a day and night of equal length

Levant: the region east of the Mediterranean Sea including Israel, Syria, Jordan, Lebanon, and Palestine

mythological: based on myths, which are traditional stories that try to explain how something came to be

periscope: a device designed for observing from a concealed position, such as underwater or around a corner

pharaoh: an ancient Egyptian king

philologist: a person who studies language through ancient texts

psychic: a person believed to have extreme mental powers, such as the ability to predict the future or communicate with the dead

remote sensing: technologies that examine objects without coming into contact with them, such as satellites, seismographs, radar, and ultrasound

solstice: one of two days each year marking the sun's lowest or highest point in the sky; the longest or shortest days of the year

stela: a stone slab or pillar with an inscription

Selected Bibliography

El-Baz, Farouk. "Gifts of the Desert." *Archaeology Magazine*. Archaeology Institute of America, Vol. 54, no. 2: March/April 2001.

Hawass, Zahi. *The Secrets of the Sphinx: Restoration Past and Present*. Cairo, Egypt: American University in Cairo Press, 1998.

Lehner, Mark, and Zahi Hawass. "The Sphinx: Who Built it, and Why?" *Archaeology Magazine*. Archaeology Institute of America, Vol. 47, no. 5: September/October 1994.

Schneider, Thomas. *Ancient Egypt in 101 Questions and Answers*. Translated by David Lorton. Edited by J. J. Shirley. Ithaca, N.Y.: Cornell University Press, 2013.

Schoch, Robert M. *Voyages of the Pyramid Builders: The True Origins of the Pyramids, from Lost Egypt to Ancient America*. With Robert Aquinas McNally. New York: Putnam, 2003.

Zivie-Coche, Christiane. *Sphinx: History of a Monument*. Translated by David Lorton. Ithaca, N.Y.: Cornell University Press, 2002.

Websites

ANCIENT CODE: 20 FACTS ABOUT THE GREAT SPHINX OF EGYPT
http://www.ancient-code.com/20-facts-about-the-great-sphinx-of-egypt/

DISCOVERING EGYPT
https://discoveringegypt.com/pyramids-temples-of-egypt/

Note: Every effort has been made to ensure that any websites listed above were active at the time of publication. However, because of the nature of the Internet, it is impossible to guarantee that these sites will remain active indefinitely or that their contents will not be altered.

Index